30 Day Productivity Challenge *for Authors*

Become More Productive in 5 Minutes a Day!

D'vorah Lansky, M.Ed.

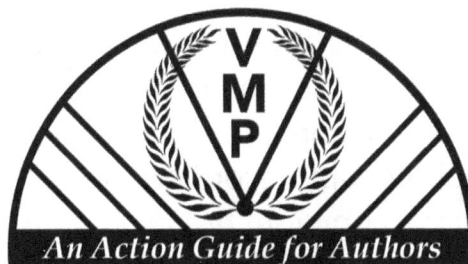

An Action Guide for Authors

Vibrant Marketing Publications
Hartford, CT

Published by Vibrant Marketing Publications
Copyright ©2016 D'vorah Lansky

www.ActionGuidesForAuthors.com

ISBN 978-0-9967431-1-2

Dedication

This book is dedicated to the amazing, success-focused authors in our 30-Day Productivity Challenge.

Your dedication and determination to achieving your dreams is inspiring.

It is a privelage and an honor to be on this success journey with you!

Become More Productive in 5 Minutes a Day!

Table of Contents and 30-Day Checklist

How to Use This Action Guide

Welcome to the 30-Day Productivity Challenge for Authors Action Guide! Over the course of 30 days, you'll discover powerful ways to become more productive, overcome overwhelm, and get more organized.

In this guide you'll find a 30-Day Action Plan along with corresponding activity pages, which I refer to as "tracking sheets." Each day, read through that day's action step and then turn to the cooresponding tracking sheets. For the most part, the daily action steps are designed in a way that will allow you to take action in about five minutes a day.

At the end of each day, circle back to this action guide to share your reflections and daily accomplishments. This will allow you to chart your progress and journal your experience.

To make the most of this program, schedule a recurring appointment, in your calendar, as your *take action time*. By focusing on this productivity challenge at the same time each day, you'll create consistency. By treating this appointment as you would an appointment with your best client, you'll accomplish a great deal.

When selecting a time to schedule into your calendar, select a time that you'll realistically be able dedicate to going through that day's action step. This will allow you to prioritize becoming more productive.

As far as mapping out your 30 days, you can choose to focus on this challenge on as many days of the week as you'd like. For consistency and to create momentum, it's recommended that you commit to 5 or 6 days a week, and that you are consistent. Over the course of this challenge, you'll be able to navigate your way through the entire 30-Day Productivity Challenge program!

Have fun with this and get ready to become more productive and organized!

Wishing you much success!

F.O.C.U.S. For Increased Productivity

Fine Tune Your Master Projects List

Optimize Your Email

Concentrate on the Essentials

Unplug and Take Time to Recharge

Streamline Your Social Media Systems

30-Day Productivity Challenge At-A-Glance

Complete the daily action steps and check them off once completed.
Refer to the daily tutorials for tips and instructions.

Focus for Days 1-6: **F**ine Tune Your Projects List

○	○	○	○	○	○
Get Clear on My "Why" Notes:	Gather Up My To-Do Lists Notes:	Create a Brain Dump Page Notes:	Choose Specific Project Notes:	Write Someday Maybes Notes:	Calendar the Brain Dump Notes:

Focus for Days 7-12: **O**ptimize Your Email

○	○	○	○	○	○
Take Note of Email Habits Notes:	Schedule Email Time Notes:	Streamline Email Box Notes:	Clean Out My Email Inbox Notes:	Enjoy My Reading Plle Notes:	Develop New Email Habits Notes:

Focus for Days 13-18: **C**oncentrate on the Essentials

○	○	○	○	○	○
Find Where Time is Spent Notes:	Find Tasks to Delegate Notes:	Make 6-Most To-Do Lists Notes:	Make Writing a Priority Notes:	Set Author Office Hours Notes:	Color-Code My Calendar Notes:

Focus for Days 19-24: **U**nplug and Take Time to Recharge

○	○	○	○	○	○
Make Time to Enjoy Life Notes:	Make Time for Me Notes:	Make Time for People Notes:	Write About Gratitude Notes:	Move My Body Notes:	Take Time to Dream Notes:

Focus for Days 25-30: **S**treamline Your Social Media Systems

○	○	○	○	○	○
Streamline Social Media Notes:	Create Twitter Lists Notes:	Automate Hootsuite Notes:	Share on Facebook Notes:	Make Time to Socialize Notes:	Enjoy Open Ended Time Notes:

9

Days 1-6

Fine Tune Your Projects List

Notes

Week-at-a-Glance Six-Most-Important Things To-Do List

Day of the Week: _____

- ☐ _____
- ☐ _____
- ☐ _____
- ☐ _____
- ☐ _____
- ☐ _____

☐Exercise   ☐Drink Water
☐Have Fun   ☐Daily Reflections Journal

Day of the Week: _____

- ☐ _____
- ☐ _____
- ☐ _____
- ☐ _____
- ☐ _____
- ☐ _____

☐Exercise   ☐Drink Water
☐Have Fun   ☐Daily Reflections Journal

Day of the Week: _____

- ☐ _____
- ☐ _____
- ☐ _____
- ☐ _____
- ☐ _____
- ☐ _____

☐Exercise   ☐Drink Water
☐Have Fun   ☐Daily Reflections Journal

Day of the Week: _____

- ☐ _____
- ☐ _____
- ☐ _____
- ☐ _____
- ☐ _____
- ☐ _____

☐Exercise   ☐Drink Water
☐Have Fun   ☐Daily Reflections Journal

Day of the Week: _____

- ☐ _____
- ☐ _____
- ☐ _____
- ☐ _____
- ☐ _____
- ☐ _____

☐Exercise   ☐Drink Water
☐Have Fun   ☐Daily Reflections Journal

Day of the Week: _____

- ☐ _____
- ☐ _____
- ☐ _____
- ☐ _____
- ☐ _____
- ☐ _____

☐Exercise ☐Drink Water ☐Have Fun
☐Daily Reflections Journal

Today's Action Step Date: _____

Day 1: Get Clear on Your "Why"

Welcome to Day 1 of the 30-Day Productivity Challenge! Today's action step revolves around identifying your "why" for wanting to become more productive. This will provide you with motiviation as you begin this 30-day journey.

Locate the *Productivity Accelerator* sheet, by turning the page. Find somewhere quiet where you can focus, and answer the questions on that page. This will help to provide you with focus and clarity on your 30-Day Productivity Challenge journey.

Turn the page for today's action pages.

At the end of the day, journal your *Daily Reflections* on the facing page. By prioritizing time to take action and reflect on your activity and results each day, you'll maximize the benefits you'll receive from this 30-Day Challenge.

Thought of the Day

"Dreams are today's answers to tomorrow's questions."
—Edgar Cayce

My Daily Reflections Journal
Day#____   Date: _____

The Best Part of My Day: _____

_____

_____

_____

_____

Something New I Learned Today: _____

_____

_____

_____

_____

3 Things I'm Grateful For Today

○ _____

○ _____

○ _____

Notes and Realizations

My Big Picture Dreams and Goals

Productivity Accelerator

Get Clear on Your "Why" for Wanting to Become More Productive

What is the primary reason you'd like to become more productive?

_____

_____

_____

What is your big-picture dream for your life and/or business?

_____

_____

_____

What is your biggest challenge, in regards to being productive?

_____

_____

_____

What is your biggest challenge in regards to being organized?

_____

_____

_____

What would you most like to accomplish in the next 30 days?

_____

_____

_____

Day 2: Gather Up All Your To-Do Lists

Welcome to Day 2 of the 30-Day Productivity Challenge! Today's Action Step is to gather up all your to-do lists, ideas, and sticky notes.

You can then attach them to a clipboard, set them on your desk on top of a piece of paper, or attach them to the *To-Do List Pages* tracking sheet. You can also take this opportunity to jot down ideas and to-do items that you've been keeping in your mind. Tomorrow we will draw from these lists to create a *Master Brain Dump Page*.

Turn the page for today's action pages.

At the end of the day, journal your *Daily Reflections* on the facing page. By prioritizing time to take action and reflect on your activity and results each day, you'll maximize the benefits you'll receive from this 30-Day Challenge.

Thought of the Day

"Every character is asking: 'What's my place?
Why am I here? I don't want the answer to be
'Just because.' You find your own purpose.
Each finds the reason to be here and how to contribute."
—Sharon Creech

18

My Daily Reflections Journal
Day#_____   Date: _____

The Best Part of My Day: _____

_____

_____

_____

_____

Something New I Learned Today: _____

_____

_____

_____

_____

3 Things I'm Grateful For Today

○ _____

○ _____

○ _____

Notes and Realizations

Gather Up Your To-Do Lists & Ideas and Attach Them to These To-Do List Pages

Gather Up Your To-Do Lists & Ideas and Attach Them to These To-Do List Pages

Day 3: Plug Your To-Do Lists into a Brain Dump Page

Welcome to Day 3 of the 30-Day Productivity Challenge! Today's action step is to take all of your to-do lists and plug them into one central location.

Turn to the *Master Brain Dump Page* and plug your to-do lists into categorized sections on the page. Once you've transferred your to-do lists to the brain dump page, you can then get rid of them, or place them in a folder and set the folder aside. You may want to make a copy of this brain dump page so you can clip it to a clipboard.

Turn the page for today's action pages.

At the end of the day, journal your *Daily Reflections* on the facing page. By prioritizing time to take action and reflect on your activity and results each day, you'll maximize the benefits you'll receive from this 30-Day Challenge.

Thought of the Day

*"What you do today
can improve all your tomorrows."*
—Ralph Marston

My Daily Reflections Journal
Day#_____   Date: _____

The Best Part of My Day: _____

_____

_____

_____

_____

Something New I Learned Today: _____

_____

_____

_____

_____

3 Things I'm Grateful For Today

O _____

O _____

O _____

Notes and Realizations

23

My Brain Dump Page

For the Month of: _____ Year: _____

Business ASAP List	Personal ASAP List	Current Main Project
Speaking Activities	**Writing Projects**	**Marketing Activities**
Reading List	**Courses to Study**	**To-Do Someday Maybe**

My Brain Dump Page

For the Month of: _____ Year: _____

25

Day 4: Create a Specific Project Brain Dump Page

Welcome to Day 4 of the 30-Day Productivity Challenge! Today's action step is to create a brain dump page for a specific project.

Yesterday you created your *Master Brain Dump Page*. While the brain dump exercise works wonderfully for your master list of to-do items, you can also create a brain dump page for specific projects. This will allow you to break down the tasks and activities required to complete those projects. Decide on one specific project that you'll focus on during this 30-day challenge. Capture your ideas by plugging them into the *Brain Dump Page for a Specific Project*.

Turn the page for today's action pages.

At the end of the day, journal your *Daily Reflections* on the facing page. By prioritizing time to take action and reflect on your activity and results each day, you'll maximize the benefits you'll receive from this 30-Day Challenge.

Thought of the Day

"Trust yourself. Create the kind of self that you will be happy to live with all your life. Make the most of yourself by fanning the tiny, inner sparks of possibility into flames of achievement."
—*Golda Meir*

My Daily Reflections Journal
Day#_____   Date: _____

The Best Part of My Day: _____

_____

_____

_____

_____

Something New I Learned Today: _____

_____

_____

_____

_____

3 Things I'm Grateful For Today

○ _____

○ _____

○ _____

Notes and Realizations

27

Brain Dump Page for a Specific Project

Project Description: _____

Brain Dump Page for a Specific Project

Project Description: _____

		29

Today's Action Step   Date: _____

Day 5: Create a Someday Maybe Page

Welcome to Day 5 of the 30-Day Productivity Challenge! Today's action step is to create a *Someday Maybe* page.

Identify to-do items and ideas that you don't see yourself focusing at this time and move them to a *Someday Maybe* page. This will allow you to capture ideas and remove them from your line of vision. Print off the *Someday Maybe* page and list items that you'd rather not think about for the foreseeable future. This way you'll have them written down but they won't take up room on your active to-do lists or brain dump pages.

Turn the page for today's action pages.

At the end of the day, journal your *Daily Reflections* on the facing page. By prioritizing time to take action and reflect on your activity and results each day, you'll maximize the benefits you'll receive from this 30-Day Challenge.

Thought of the Day

"What you get by achieving your goals is not as important as what you become by achieving your goals."
—Zig Ziglar

My Daily Reflections Journal
Day#_____   Date: _____

The Best Part of My Day: _____

_____

_____

_____

_____

Something New I Learned Today: _____

_____

_____

_____

_____

3 Things I'm Grateful For Today

○ _____

○ _____

○ _____

Notes and Realizations

31

My Someday Maybe Page

Plug in items here that you may want to get to someday, maybe!

Wish List	Reading List	Project List

My Someday Maybe Page

Plug in items here that you may want to get to someday, maybe!

Day 6: Calendar Your Brain Dump Pages

Welcome to Day 6 of the 30-Day Productivity Challenge! Today's action step is to pull items from your brain dump pages and plug them into your calendar.

You can use the *Monthly Calendar Page* for easy access, or you can plug things directly into your main calendar. In either case, you'll want to actually schedule items into your main calendar. This activity will help you to create a laser focus and will allow you to take a lot off your plate, for this time period. Prioritize what you'll be working on this month and decide what would be better to get to in future months.

Turn the page for today's action pages.

At the end of the day, journal your *Daily Reflections* on the facing page. By prioritizing time to take action and reflect on your activity and results each day, you'll maximize the benefits you'll receive from this 30-Day Challenge.

Thought of the Day

"Learn from yesterday, live for today, hope for tomorrow. The important thing is not to stop questioning."
—Albert Einstein

My Daily Reflections Journal
Day#_____   Date: _____

The Best Part of My Day: _____

_____

_____

_____

_____

Something New I Learned Today: _____

_____

_____

_____

_____

3 Things I'm Grateful For Today

○ _____

○ _____

○ _____

Notes and Realizations

Monthly Calendar for: Month:_____ Year:_____

(Fill in the dates for the month then plug in tasks, events, and activities.)

Monday	Tuesday	Wednesday	Thursday	Friday

36

Monthly Calendar for: Month:_____ Year:_____

(Fill in the dates for the month then plug in tasks, events, and activities.)

Monday	Tuesday	Wednesday	Thursday	Friday

37

Notes

Congratulations on Completing This Focus Area "Fine Tune Your Projects List"

Congratulations on completing Focus Area 1 of the 30-Day Productivity Challenge. These past 6 days we focused on fine tuning your projects list.

Throughout the week you had opportunities to:

- ☐ Identify your "why" for wanting to become productive
- ☐ Gather up all your to-do lists and sticky notes
- ☐ Plug your to-do items into a master brain dump page
- ☐ Create a specific project brain dump page
- ☐ Move items to a someday maybe page
- ☐ Pull items from your brain dump pages and plug them into your calendar.

How does it feel to get clear on your "why" and on your goals? _____

_____

_____

How does it feel to organize your to-do lists, ideas, and have them in one location?

_____

_____

What excites you most about becoming more productive? _____

_____

_____

Hot Tip

If you have not yet had the chance to complete all of the action steps from the previous 6 days, schedule time to do so before going on to our next focus area. This will allow you to lay a solid foundation towards becoming more productive. Consider scheduling daily time in your calendar, so you can dedicate a few minutes each day to take action towards becoming more productive.

Days
7-12

Optimize Your Email

Notes

Week-at-a-Glance Six-Most-Important Things To-Do List

Day of the Week: _____

- ☐ _____
- ☐ _____
- ☐ _____
- ☐ _____
- ☐ _____
- ☐ _____

☐Exercise ☐Drink Water
☐Have Fun ☐Daily Reflections Journal

Day of the Week: _____

- ☐ _____
- ☐ _____
- ☐ _____
- ☐ _____
- ☐ _____
- ☐ _____

☐Exercise ☐Drink Water
☐Have Fun ☐Daily Reflections Journal

Day of the Week: _____

- ☐ _____
- ☐ _____
- ☐ _____
- ☐ _____
- ☐ _____
- ☐ _____

☐Exercise ☐Drink Water
☐Have Fun ☐Daily Reflections Journal

Day of the Week: _____

- ☐ _____
- ☐ _____
- ☐ _____
- ☐ _____
- ☐ _____
- ☐ _____

☐Exercise ☐Drink Water
☐Have Fun ☐Daily Reflections Journal

Day of the Week: _____

- ☐ _____
- ☐ _____
- ☐ _____
- ☐ _____
- ☐ _____
- ☐ _____

☐Exercise ☐Drink Water
☐Have Fun ☐Daily Reflections Journal

Day of the Week: _____

- ☐ _____
- ☐ _____
- ☐ _____
- ☐ _____
- ☐ _____
- ☐ _____

☐Exercise ☐Drink Water ☐Have Fun
☐Daily Reflections Journal

Today's Action Step   Date: _____

Day 7: Become Aware of Your Email Habits

Welcome to Day 7 of the 30-Day Productivity Challenge! Today's action step is to become aware of your email habits.

Email is a powerful tool for communicating with the people who are important in your life, but if you are not careful, it can also become a major source of distraction. The first step in streamlining your email habits is to become aware of how much time is being spent checking email each day. Refer to the *Email Reality Check Page* and track your email habits. Each time you check your email, make note of the time and how long you spend checking email.

Turn the page for today's action pages.

At the end of the day, journal your *Daily Reflections* on the facing page. By prioritizing time to take action and reflect on your activity and results each day, you'll maximize the benefits you'll receive from this 30-Day Challenge.

Thought of the Day

"One look at an email can rob you of 15 minutes of focus."
—Jacqueline Leo

My Daily Reflections Journal
Day#_____   Date: _____

The Best Part of My Day: _____

_____

_____

_____

_____

Something New I Learned Today: _____

_____

_____

_____

_____

3 Things I'm Grateful For Today

○ _____

○ _____

○ _____

Notes and Realizations

Email Reality Check #1   Date: _____

Track How Often and How Much Time You Spend Checking Email

Start Time	End Time	Total Time Spent
- - - - -	**Grand Total >>>**	

Notes and Realizations

_____

_____

_____

Email Reality Check #2   Date: _____

Track How Often and How Much Time You Spend Checking Email

Start Time	End Time	Total Time Spent
- - - - -	**Grand Total >>>**	

Notes and Realizations

_____

_____

_____

_____

_____

_____

Day 8: Schedule Times to Check Your Email

Welcome to Day 8 of the 30-Day Productivity Challenge! Today's action step is to schedule times to check email.

When we check email, whenever the mood strikes us or whenever we hear a ping or a ring, it's very easy to get distracted. To tame the email dragon and reclaim your day, schedule specific times during the day to check your email. By doing this, you will free up a great deal of time and you will be able to concentrate, uninterrupted, on essential tasks and projects. The trick is, you'll want to discipline yourself to check your email only at scheduled times.

Turn the page for today's action pages.

At the end of the day, journal your *Daily Reflections* on the facing page. By prioritizing time to take action and reflect on your activity and results each day, you'll maximize the benefits you'll receive from this 30-Day Challenge.

Thought of the Day

"I learned not to confuse 'busy' with 'productive,'
but I'm still far too addicted to email to resist
its early-morning digital snuggles."
—Chris Hardwick

My Daily Reflections Journal
Day#_____   Date: _____

The Best Part of My Day: _____

_____

_____

_____

_____

Something New I Learned Today: _____

_____

_____

_____

_____

3 Things I'm Grateful For Today

○ _____

○ _____

○ _____

Notes and Realizations

Tips for Taming the Email Dragon
Contributed by Members of Our Author Community

"Use one email account strictly for business communications, use another for online purchases, newsletters, and opt-in lists. This way, you can isolate critical communications from the rest."

—Chris, NY

"I suggest picking two times during the day to check email and to only do it at those specified times. Avoid checking email during the first two hours of your business day because those are the most productive hours. Once you decide the times, decide on a duration limit, such as 15 minutes, and then stick to it. As you become aware of the time you spend on responding to emails, you'll become more efficient."

—Glenn, CT

"Look at the time. Awareness is the first key to making any beneficial change. Literally, clocking yourself from the beginning of an "email session" to the end will bring insight for you. You can then decide if your time has been well spent, or if you are wasting it."

—Sue, NJ

"One of the most efficient ways I've found to "tame the email dragon" is to use email filters to sift through the incoming email and deposit it into folders which have priorities set for them.

- Things that are marked as important get looked at sooner.
- Other items will be looked at towards the end of the day.
- If something is really important there are more effective ways of reaching someone other than sending them an email."

—Michael, AZ

My Email Checking Schedule

It takes 21 days to create a new habit. Schedule specific times to check your email each day. Set these as recuring appointments in your calendar, for the next three weeks or longer. You may want to check your email less often, or not at all, on the weekends. You know best what will work for you and your lifestyle.

Plug email checking times into your calendar, and track your email checking habits for the next 21 days. The easiset way to develop a new habit is to schedule it at the same time each day.

What Times of the Day Will You Check Your Email During the Week?

My Email Checking Schedule

What Times of the Day Will You Check Your Email Over the Weekend?

My Email Checking Schedule

Today's Action Step   Date: _____

Day 9: Streamline Your Email Box

Welcome to Day 9 of the 30-Day Productivity Challenge! Today's action step is to streamline your email box by creating folders or labels.

This will allow you to more easily locate messages. Creating folders or labels for your email box will also reduce the number of emails you have in your email box. Develop the habit of filing your email as soon as you've read and responded to a message. Having a clean email box is like having a clean desk and will help you to feel less overwhelmed while allowing you to become more productive.

Turn the page for today's action pages.

At the end of the day, journal your *Daily Reflections* on the facing page. By prioritIzing time to take action and reflect on your activity and results each day, you'll maximize the benefits you'll receive from this 30-Day Challenge.

Thought of the Day

"I have three desks. One empty for paperwork, one for the Internet and email, and one for the writing computer."
—Lee Child

My Daily Reflections Journal
Day#_____   Date: _____

The Best Part of My Day: _____

_____

_____

_____

_____

Something New I Learned Today: _____

_____

_____

_____

_____

3 Things I'm Grateful For Today

○ _____

○ _____

○ _____

Notes and Realizations

Create Folders and Labels for Your Email

Filing your email into folders or tagging it with labels, allows you to reduce the amount of email you have in your inbox and makes it easier for you to find specific messages in the future.

Here Are Examples of Titles for Email Folders or Labels.

Admin	Friends and Family	Study ASAP
Books to Read	My Books	Subscriptions
Coaching Clients	Reading Pile	Travel
Courses I'm Taking	Receipts	Virtual Team

List Examples of Folders or Labels You Can Add to Your Email Program

_____   _____

_____   _____

_____   _____

_____   _____

_____   _____

How will filing your messages help you to become more productive?

_____

_____

_____

Taming the Email Dragon Journal

Journal your thoughts, ideas, and realizations.

How does it feel to be gaining control of your email box? _____

_____

_____

What is it like to be able to focus on things without the distraction of email?

_____

_____

As you develop new email habits, what realizations do you have?

_____

_____

What is one thing you can do to further tame the email dragon?

_____

_____

Notes

_____

_____

_____

_____

_____

_____

_____

Today's Action Step

Day 10: Clean Out Your Inbox Each Week

Welcome to Day 10 of the 30-Day Productivity Challenge! Today's action step is to take time to clean out your inbox.

By clearing out your inbox, you'll reduce overwhelm and you'll be able to easily access important emails that require action or a response. Begin the practice of cleaning out your inbox at the end of each week. Use this time to unsubscribe from subscriptions no longer relevant, file emails into folders, respond to emails needing a response, delete junk email, and tag emails that you'll address when you get back to your computer on Monday.

Turn the page for today's action pages.

At the end of the day, journal your *Daily Reflections* on the facing page. By prioritizing time to take action and reflect on your activity and results each day, you'll maximize the benefits you'll receive from this 30-Day Challenge.

Thought of the Day

"I think it's nice sometimes not to be plugged in 24/7 to email and the Internet and everything else. It's nice to get away."
—Andrew Luck

My Daily Reflections Journal
Day#_____   Date: _____

The Best Part of My Day: _____

_____

_____

_____

_____

Something New I Learned Today: _____

_____

_____

_____

_____

3 Things I'm Grateful For Today

○ _____

○ _____

○ _____

Notes and Realizations

Tips to Help You Clean Out Your Inbox

Here Are a Few Tips to Help You Get Started

- ☐ Schedule time at the end of each week to clear out your inbox

- ☐ Unsubscribe from subscriptions that are no longer relevant

- ☐ Delete your junk mail and messages you know you won't be reading

- ☐ Add items to your reading pile folder

- ☐ Color code fun items you'd like to enjoy over the weekend

- ☐ Respond to any urgent or time sensitive messages and then file them

- ☐ Color code messages you'll be addressing at the beginning of the week

What other ideas come to mind to help you clean out your email inbox?

_____

_____

_____

Taming the Email Dragon Journal

Journal Your Thoughts, Ideas, and Realizations

How does it feel to be gaining control of your email box? _____

_____

_____

_____

How does it feel to know that you can easily access your reading pile? _____

_____

_____

_____

What does it feel like to have a clutter-free inbox? _____

_____

_____

_____

My Thoughts and Ideas

_____

_____

_____

_____

_____

_____

_____

_____

Day 11: Take Time to Enjoy Your Reading Pile

Welcome to Day 11 of the 30-Day Productivity Challenge! Today's action step is to schedule time to enjoy content in your "reading pile" folder.

When you receive emails that don't require immediate action and are ones that you want to be able to read through and enjoy, tag them and place them in your reading pile folder. Schedule at least one time a week when you'll take time to enjoy these messages in your reading pile. You may find that week-ends or evenings are a perfect time for this type of enjoyable activity.

Turn the page for today's action pages.

At the end of the day, journal your *Daily Reflections* on the facing page. By prioritizing time to take action and reflect on your activity and results each day, you'll maximize the benefits you'll receive from this 30-Day Challenge.

Thought of the Day

"He that loves reading has everything within his reach."
—William GodwinRead

My Daily Reflections Journal
Day#_____   Date: _____

The Best Part of My Day: _____

_____

_____

_____

_____

Something New I Learned Today: _____

_____

_____

_____

_____

3 Things I'm Grateful For Today

○ _____

○ _____

○ _____

Notes and Realizations

Schedule Time to Enjoy Your Reading Pile

Schedule one or more times a week to enjoy your reading pile. These are emails that you know you'd enjoy, personally or professionally. Typically reading pile emails consist of email newsletters and interesting articles. They could also be email which include a link to an intereseting website that you'd like to take time to explore.

Open up your calendar and schedule one or more times a week to enjoy your reading pile. Set this as a recurring appointment so you create consistency.

When do you have it scheduled to enjoy your email box reading pile?

Day of Week: _____   Time of Day: _____

Day of Week: _____   Time of Day: _____

Day of Week: _____   Time of Day: _____

Open up your reading pile folder and write down the titles or topics of the first 3 emails you'll read from your reading pile.

Topic of Email or Article: _____

Person Who Sent Email or Wrote Article: _____

Topic of Email or Article: _____

Person Who Sent Email or Wrote Article: _____

Topic of Email or Article: _____

Person Who Sent Email or Wrote Article: _____

Capture Inspiring Content

Here's a Place to Take Notes and Write Down Recommended Strategies,
Inspiring Ideas, and Interesting Tools and Resources You'd Like to Explore

_____

_____

_____

_____

_____

_____

_____

_____

_____

_____

_____

_____

_____

_____

_____

_____

_____

_____

_____

Today's Action Step   Date: _____
Day 12: Develop New Email Checking Habits

Welcome to Day 12 of the 30-Day Productivity Challenge! Today's action step is to compose a list of things you can do to help you resist checking email during times other than those you've scheduled for email checking.

Developing new habits can be challenging and it takes time to settle in to new routines. Spend time writing down a list of things you can do when you feel tempted to check your email, at times other than those you've scheduled into your calendar.

Turn the page for today's action pages.

At the end of the day, journal your *Daily Reflections* on the facing page. By prioritizing time to take action and reflect on your activity and results each day, you'll maximize the benefits you'll receive from this 30-Day Challenge.

Thought of the Day

*"Watch your thoughts, for they become words.
Choose your words, for they become actions.
Understand your actions, for they become habits.
Study your habits, for they will become your character.
Develop your character, for it becomes your destiny."*
—Unknown

My Daily Reflections Journal
Day#_____   Date: _____

The Best Part of My Day: _____

_____

_____

_____

_____

Something New I Learned Today: _____

_____

_____

_____

_____

3 Things I'm Grateful For Today

○ _____

○ _____

○ _____

Notes and Realizations

Things to Do to Help You Resist Checking Your Email

* Know that while email is an essential communication tool in your life and business, it doesn't own your time or schedule. You are the boss of your email and you can reclaim your day by setting a realistic email checking schedule.

* Know that you can refine your schedule as you determine the best schedule for you.

* If you have an urge to check email, at times other than those listed as email checking time in your calendar, try some of the following strategies:

- Look at the clock and figure out how long it is until your next scheduled email check. Then map out an action plan of what you can focus on during that time. By exercising your discipline muscle, it will become easier and easier to resist the temptation to check your email.

- As you develop this new habit, perhaps set yourself milestone rewards. For example, let's say you are writing an article or proofreading your book. Set yourself a goal of writing or proofing a certain number of pages. When tempted to check email, remind yourself that you'll be rewarded with a five or ten minute email checking break as soon as you complete the task before you.

- When the idea pops into your mind to email someone a quick question, or you remember you need to reply to an email, jot down a reminder on a pad of paper, which you can refer to the next time you to to check your email.

After Reading the Above, What Additional Ideas Come to Mind?

_____

_____

_____

Things I Can Do When I feel
Lured In By the Email Dragon

I can remember that my email checking times are at:

_____   _____

_____   _____

_____   _____

When I'm sitting at my computer, I can minimize the tempation to check email by:

_____

_____

Here are five things I can do, when I feel tempted to check email:

○ _____

○ _____

○ _____

○ _____

○ _____

Thoughts and Ideas

_____

_____

_____

_____

Notes

Congratulations on Completing This Focus Area "Optimize Your Email"

Congratulations on completing Focus Area 2 of the 30-Day Productivity Challenge. These past 6 days we focused on optimizing your email and your email habits.

Throughout the week you had opportunities to:

- ☐ Become aware of your email habits
- ☐ Schedule specific times for checking email
- ☐ Develop new habits and resist email checking
- ☐ Streamline your email box
- ☐ Schedule time to clear out your inbox
- ☐ Take time to enjoy your reading pile

How does it feel to have fine tuned your email box? _____

_____

_____

What excites you most about gaining control over your email checking habits? _____

_____

_____

What will you do to help yourself resist constantly checking email? _____

_____

_____

Hot Tip: "Set a Timer"

Your timer is your friend! You can use it to help you limit the time you spend checking email and you can use it to help you focus on your tasks at hand. When you feel an urge to check your email, at times other than those you have scheduled for this task, set your timer and then focus your attention on a specific writing or editing project. Like any positive new habit, it takes time to develop but it is worth the effort.

69

Days 13-18

Concentrate on the Esssentials

Notes

Week-at-a-Glance Six-Most-Important Things To-Do List

Day of the Week: _____

- ☐ _____
- ☐ _____
- ☐ _____
- ☐ _____
- ☐ _____
- ☐ _____

☐Exercise   ☐Drink Water
☐Have Fun   ☐Daily Reflections Journal

Day of the Week: _____

- ☐ _____
- ☐ _____
- ☐ _____
- ☐ _____
- ☐ _____
- ☐ _____

☐Exercise   ☐Drink Water
☐Have Fun   ☐Daily Reflections Journal

Day of the Week: _____

- ☐ _____
- ☐ _____
- ☐ _____
- ☐ _____
- ☐ _____
- ☐ _____

☐Exercise   ☐Drink Water
☐Have Fun   ☐Daily Reflections Journal

Day of the Week: _____

- ☐ _____
- ☐ _____
- ☐ _____
- ☐ _____
- ☐ _____
- ☐ _____

☐Exercise   ☐Drink Water
☐Have Fun   ☐Daily Reflections Journal

Day of the Week: _____

- ☐ _____
- ☐ _____
- ☐ _____
- ☐ _____
- ☐ _____
- ☐ _____

☐Exercise   ☐Drink Water
☐Have Fun   ☐Daily Reflections Journal

Day of the Week: _____

- ☐ _____
- ☐ _____
- ☐ _____
- ☐ _____
- ☐ _____
- ☐ _____

☐Exercise ☐Drink Water ☐Have Fun
☐Daily Reflections Journal

Day 13: Identify Where You Are Spending Time

Welcome to Day 13 of the 30-Day Productivity Challenge! Today's action step is to identify where you are spending your time.

Are you doing things that are of greatest benefit to you, personally and professionally, or do you find that your day is spent reacting to requests and deadlines? It's been said that, "you can begin a new habit in the middle of a bag of potato chips!" Creating good habits in one are of your life can create the discipline to create good habits in other areas of your life. What new habits would you like to incorporate into your life?

Turn the page for today's action pages.

At the end of the day, journal your *Daily Reflections* on the facing page. By prioritizing time to take action and reflect on your activity and results each day, you'll maximize the benefits you'll receive from this 30-Day Challenge.

Thought of the Day

"The future belongs to those who prepare for it today."
—Malcolm X

My Daily Reflections Journal
Day#_____   Date: _____

The Best Part of My Day: _____

_____

_____

_____

_____

Something New I Learned Today: _____

_____

_____

_____

_____

3 Things I'm Grateful For Today

- ○ _____
- ○ _____
- ○ _____

Notes and Realizations

Where Are You Spending Time   Date: _____

Pick a Day During the Week and Keep Track of Everything You Do

Activity	Start Time	End Time	Total Time
- - - - -		**Grand Total >**	

Notes and Realizations

_____

_____

_____

_____

_____

Where Are You Spending Time   Date: _____

Continue Tracking From the Previous Page or Begin Tracking a New Day

Activity	Start Time	End Time	Total Time
- - - - -		**Grand Total >**	

Notes and Realizations

_____

_____

_____

_____

_____

Today's Action Step
Date: _____

Day 14: Find Tasks to Delegate

Welcome to Day 14 of the 30-Day Productivity Challenge! Today's action step is to find ways to take things off of your plate by identifying things you can delegate to others.

To help identify which tasks you need to be focusing on and which are better outsourced, complete the exercises you'll find on today's tracking sheets. Once you've identified tasks that you either don't want to be doing or you know are ones that don't make the best use of your time, give thought to who you can outsource to. Refer to the *Creative Outsourcing Ideas* page for ideas.

Turn the page for today's action pages.

At the end of the day, journal your *Daily Reflections* on the facing page. By prioritizing time to take action and reflect on your activity and results each day, you'll maximize the benefits you'll receive from this 30-Day Challenge.

Thought of the Day

*"I either delegate something,
I dump it, or I deal with it."*
—Daniel L. Doctorof

My Daily Reflections Journal
Day#_____   Date: _____

The Best Part of My Day: _____

_____

_____

_____

_____

Something New I Learned Today: _____

_____

_____

_____

_____

3 Things I'm Grateful For Today

○ _____

○ _____

○ _____

Notes and Realizations

Tasks and Activities in My Life and Business

Refer to the *Where Are You Spending Your Time* Tracking Sheet from Day 13. Pull from that page to create a list of tasks that you must do and a list of tasks that you can outsource to someone else.

Your time is best spent doing things that you enjoy doing and those that have to do with connecting with potential clients and business contacts. Try not to give thought to how much it will cost to outsource tasks as the investment can save you time & money and there are creative and affordable options available.

Tasks I Must Do	Tasks I Can Outsource

Notes and observations as I compose this list: _____

Creative Outsourcing Ideas

Oftentimes when people think about outsourcing they think they can't afford it. The real question is, "can you afford NOT to outsource tasks that you either don't enjoy doing or you know are not the best use of your time?

A good gauge to measure whether your time is best spent on a task is to ask yourself, *"Is what I'm doing right now taking me closer to my dreams and goals?"*

If it is, then keep going. If not, then perhaps you need to refocus and save that activity for time ouside of your "office hours" or perhaps it is an activity that can be outsourced.

Possible People to Outsource To

- Family Members
- People You Know in the Business Community
- Your Clients or Students (for pay or for barter)
- College Students (for internships)
- Professionals on an Outsourcing Site Such As Fiverr.com

Complete This Chart to Help Identify Possible People To

Tasks I'd Like to Outsource	People I Can Outsource To

Day 15: Your Six-Most-Important To-Do List

Welcome to Day 15 of the 30-Day Productivity Challenge! Today's action step is to prioritize the six most important things on your to-do list.

Take back control of your day and learn to focus on what's most important. Refer to the *Six-Most-Important Things To-Do List*, by turning the page. Make it a priority to plan your day, the night before. That way you'll be prepared when you get to work so you can focus your attention on the most important tasks. You'll notice that there is room on each day's list to also track positive healthy habits. You may find having a handy daily reminder to be helpful.

Turn the page for today's action pages.

At the end of the day, journal your *Daily Reflections* on the facing page. By prioritizing time to take action and reflect on your activity and results each day, you'll maximize the benefits you'll receive from this 30-Day Challenge.

Thought of the Day

"It takes half your life before you discover life is a do-it-yourself project."
—Napoleon Hill

My Daily Reflections Journal
Day#_____   Date: _____

The Best Part of My Day: _____

_____

_____

_____

_____

Something New I Learned Today: _____

_____

_____

_____

_____

3 Things I'm Grateful For Today

○ _____

○ _____

○ _____

Notes and Realizations

Story of the Six-Most-Important Things To-Do List

You may have noticed that there is a six-most-important things to-do list at the beginning of each focus area in this action guide. Having a handy way to capture your to-do items for the week can really help you to streamline your day.

It may seem like there is a never ending list of tasks for you to complete. While that may be true, you can take control of your schedule in a way that will allow you to accomplish more than you can imagine. You can get a tremendous amount done by planning each day the night before by creating a "six most important things to do" list. This will give you a jumpstart on your day and keep you focused on what is most essential.

The concept of the six-most-important things to-do list was developed by Ivy Lee, a well-known efficiency expert in the early 1900's. The story goes, that Ivy Lee approached Charles Schwab, owner of Bethlehem Steel.

In the early 1900s, Charles Schwab, President of Bethlehem Steel, wanted to increase his own efficiency, and that of the management team at the steel company. Ivy Lee, a well-known efficiency expert of the time, approached Mr. Schwab, and made a proposition Charles Schwab could not refuse. Ivy Lee said that he could increase his peoples' efficiency and his company's sales if Schwab would allow him to spend fifteen minutes with each of his executives. Charles Schwab asked him how much it would cost him. Ivy Lee replied: "Nothing, unless it works. After three months, you can send me a check for whatever you feel it's worth to you." Charles Schwab agreed and told him he had a deal.

The next day Ivy Lee met individually, with each of the management executive. He instructed them to spend time at the end of each day, for ninety days, to compose a list of the six most important things that they'd focus on the following day and to number the items in their order of importance."

They asked if that was it and Ivy Lee responded with: "That's it. Check off each item after finishing it, and go on to the next item on your list. If something doesn't get done, put it on the following day's list."

Each of the executives agreed to follow Ivy Lee's instructions. Three months later, Charles Schwab studied the results and was so pleased that he sent Lee a check for $35,000! (That's $35,000 in the early 1900's!)

Week-at-a-Glance Six-Most-Important Things To-Do List

Day of the Week: _____

- ☐ _____
- ☐ _____
- ☐ _____
- ☐ _____
- ☐ _____
- ☐ _____

☐Exercise ☐Drink Water
☐Have Fun ☐Daily Reflections Journal

Day of the Week: _____

- ☐ _____
- ☐ _____
- ☐ _____
- ☐ _____
- ☐ _____
- ☐ _____

☐Exercise ☐Drink Water
☐Have Fun ☐Daily Reflections Journal

Day of the Week: _____

- ☐ _____
- ☐ _____
- ☐ _____
- ☐ _____
- ☐ _____
- ☐ _____

☐Exercise ☐Drink Water
☐Have Fun ☐Daily Reflections Journal

Day of the Week: _____

- ☐ _____
- ☐ _____
- ☐ _____
- ☐ _____
- ☐ _____
- ☐ _____

☐Exercise ☐Drink Water
☐Have Fun ☐Daily Reflections Journal

Day of the Week: _____

- ☐ _____
- ☐ _____
- ☐ _____
- ☐ _____
- ☐ _____
- ☐ _____

☐Exercise ☐Drink Water
☐Have Fun ☐Daily Reflections Journal

Day of the Week: _____

- ☐ _____
- ☐ _____
- ☐ _____
- ☐ _____
- ☐ _____
- ☐ _____

☐Exercise ☐Drink Water ☐Have Fun
☐Daily Reflections Journal

Day 16: Make Writing a Priority

Welcome to Day 16 of the 30-Day Productivity Challenge! Today's action step is to find ways to make writing a priority.

As a success-focused author, it is essential that you focus on writing, on a regular basis. Harness the power of this week's focus to carve out time, at least a few times each week, for writing. Writing can consist of writing your book, writing blog posts or articles, writing email messages to your subscribers, and writing marketing materials. Think of how much you can accomplish if you give your writing time a "front seat" on your calendar.

Turn the page for today's action pages.

At the end of the day, journal your *Daily Reflections* on the facing page. By prioritizing time to take action and reflect on your activity and results each day, you'll maximize the benefits you'll receive from this 30-Day Challenge.

Thought of the Day

"It is the set of the sails, not the direction of the wind that determines which way we go."
—Jim Rohn

My Daily Reflections Journal
Day#_____   Date: _____

The Best Part of My Day: _____

_____

_____

_____

_____

Something New I Learned Today: _____

_____

_____

_____

_____

3 Things I'm Grateful For Today

O _____

O _____

O _____

Notes and Realizations

I Make Writing a Priority in My Life
Give Thought to the Types of Things You'd Like to Write About

I've looked at my calendar and have found time(s) that I can dedicate to writing. I have these scheduled as recurring appointments in my calendar.

My Writing Times

Day of Week: _____   Time of Day: _____

Day of Week: _____   Time of Day: _____

Day of Week: _____   Time of Day: _____

3 Topics I'd Like to Write About

- ○ _____
- ○ _____
- ○ _____

How Does it Feel Knowing You've Scheduled Time for Writing?

_____

_____

_____

What Can You Do to Safeguard and Prioritize This Precious Writing Time?

_____

_____

Sketch Out Your Writing Ideas

Writing Idea #1: _____

_____

_____

_____

_____

_____

_____

Writing Idea #2: _____

_____

_____

_____

_____

_____

_____

Writing Idea #3: _____

_____

_____

_____

_____

_____

_____

Today's Action Step

Day 17: Set Author Office Hours

Welcome to Day 17 of the 30-Day Productivity Challenge! Today's action step is to schedule your author office hours.

Setting author office hours will empower you and allow you to accomplish more. Posting your hours, so they are visible to the people in your home or office, will also help to reduce distractions. As you map out your author office hours, be sure to set yourself up for success so you can prioritize this time and not push it to the side when something comes up. Short of an emergency, treat your author office hours as you would treat time with your best client.

Turn the page for today's action pages.

At the end of the day, journal your *Daily Reflections* on the facing page. By prioritizing time to take action and reflect on your activity and results each day, you'll maximize the benefits you'll receive from this 30-Day Challenge.

Thought of the Day

"A year from now you will wish you had started today."
—Karen Lamb

My Daily Reflections Journal
Day#_____   Date: _____

The Best Part of My Day: _____

_____

_____

_____

_____

Something New I Learned Today: _____

_____

_____

_____

_____

3 Things I'm Grateful For Today

○ _____

○ _____

○ _____

Notes and Realizations

My Author Office Hours

Schedule times to focus on content creation, marketing, and other areas of your life as an author. Plug these times into your main calendar as recurring appointments.

Prioritize this time and don't push it to the side when something comes up. Short of an emergency, treat your author office hours as you would time with your best client.

Plug in the times of day down the first column and the days of the week along the first row. This will allow you to set the starting and ending time of your day and the days of the week that you'll work on your author business.

↓Time | Days →					

Things to Focus on During Author Office Hours

Use this page to capture ideas for what you'll focus on during Author Office Hours.

Writing

Editing

Marketing

Planning

93

Day 18: Color-Code Your Calendar

Welcome to Day 18 of the 30-Day Productivity Challenge! Today's action step is to color-code your calendar.

By doing this you will be able to tell, at a glance, when you have scheduled phone calls, when you need to be out-of-the-office, which activities are family activities, when your writing time is, etc. The first thing you'll want to do is create a color code. In your mind, which colors relate to which activities. You can color-code a physical calendar by using highlighter markers. You can also color code your Outlook or Google calendar by using their color-coded categories.

Turn the page for today's action pages.

At the end of the day, journal your *Daily Reflections* on the facing page. By prioritizing time to take action and reflect on your activity and results each day, you'll maximize the benefits you'll receive from this 30-Day Challenge.

Thought of the Day

"Your greatest resource is your time."
—Brian Tracy

My Daily Reflections Journal
Day#_____   Date: _____

The Best Part of My Day: _____

_____

_____

_____

_____

Something New I Learned Today: _____

_____

_____

_____

_____

3 Things I'm Grateful For Today

○ _____

○ _____

○ _____

Notes and Realizations

Color-Code Your Author Activities

Plug in the times of day down the first column and the days of the week along the first row, that you work on your author business. Then take highlighter pens and color code your activities so you can see what you are doing, at a glance.

My Color Code - Example: Red = Scheduled Phone Call

Color: _____ = _____   Color: _____ = _____

Color: _____ = _____   Color: _____ = _____

Color: _____ = _____   Color: _____ = _____

↓Time | Days →					
96					

Color-Code Your Personal and Work Activities

Plug in the times of day down the first column and the days of the week along the first row, that you work on your author business. Then take highlighter pens and color code your activities so you can see what you are doing, at a glance.

My Color Code - Example: Red = Scheduled Phone Call

Color: _____ = _____   Color: _____ = _____

Color: _____ = _____   Color: _____ = _____

Color: _____ = _____   Color: _____ = _____

↓Time | Days →				

97

Notes

Congratulations on Completing This Focus Area "Concentrate on the Essentials"

Congratulations on completing Focus Area 3 of the 30-Day Productivity Challenge. These past 6 days we focused on concentrating on the essentials.

Throughout the week you had opportunities to:

- ☐ Identify where you are spending time
- ☐ Find tasks to delegate
- ☐ Create your six-most-important things to-do list
- ☐ Make writing a priority
- ☐ Schedule office hours
- ☐ Color-code your calendar

How does it feel to know where you are spending your time? _____

_____

_____

Which tasks will you be ousourcing? _____

_____

_____

How can you harness the power of the "Six Most Important Things To-Do List? _____

_____

_____

Hot Tip: "Plan for Tomorrow"

At the end of each day, check things off of your to-do list, move uncompleted items to the following day's to-do list and prepare your six-most-important list for the following day. This one act can help make your tomorrows more productive, as you'll arrive to work knowing what you'll be focusing on. You may find it helpful to use the *Week-at-a-Glance* lists (found at the start of each focus area) so you can plug in to-do items on days that you know you'll be able to get to those tasks.

Days
19-24

Unplug and Take Time to Recharge

Notes

Week-at-a-Glance Six-Most-Important Things To-Do List

Day of the Week: _____

- ☐ _____
- ☐ _____
- ☐ _____
- ☐ _____
- ☐ _____
- ☐ _____

☐Exercise   ☐Drink Water
☐Have Fun   ☐Daily Reflections Journal

Day of the Week: _____

- ☐ _____
- ☐ _____
- ☐ _____
- ☐ _____
- ☐ _____
- ☐ _____

☐Exercise   ☐Drink Water
☐Have Fun   ☐Daily Reflections Journal

Day of the Week: _____

- ☐ _____
- ☐ _____
- ☐ _____
- ☐ _____
- ☐ _____
- ☐ _____

☐Exercise   ☐Drink Water
☐Have Fun   ☐Daily Reflections Journal

Day of the Week: _____

- ☐ _____
- ☐ _____
- ☐ _____
- ☐ _____
- ☐ _____
- ☐ _____

☐Exercise   ☐Drink Water
☐Have Fun   ☐Daily Reflections Journal

Day of the Week: _____

- ☐ _____
- ☐ _____
- ☐ _____
- ☐ _____
- ☐ _____
- ☐ _____

☐Exercise   ☐Drink Water
☐Have Fun   ☐Daily Reflections Journal

Day of the Week: _____

- ☐ _____
- ☐ _____
- ☐ _____
- ☐ _____
- ☐ _____
- ☐ _____

☐Exercise ☐Drink Water ☐Have Fun
☐Daily Reflections Journal

Day 19: Make Time to Enjoy Life

Welcome to Day 19 of the 30-Day Productivity Challenge! Today's action step is to find ways to unplug, recharge, and make time to enjoy life.

It is important that you take time to unplug and time to recharge. This will give you renewed energy for your work, writing, family, friends, and other areas of your life. Refer to the *Things You Can Do to Recharge Your Batteries* tracking sheet and get excited! Making it a priority to have fun and enjoy life will enrich you in many ways!

Turn the page for today's action pages.

At the end of the day, journal your *Daily Reflections* on the facing page. By prioritizing time to take action and reflect on your activity and results each day, you'll maximize the benefits you'll receive from this 30-Day Challenge.

Thought of the Day

"The biggest adventure you can ever take is to live the life of your dreams."
—Oprah Winfrey

My Daily Reflections Journal
Day#_____   Date: _____

The Best Part of My Day: _____

_____

_____

_____

_____

Something New I Learned Today: _____

_____

_____

_____

_____

3 Things I'm Grateful For Today

○ _____

○ _____

○ _____

Notes and Realizations

Doodle - Brainstorm - Daydream

Things You Can Do To Recharge Your Batteries

What do you love doing?

○ _____

○ _____

○ _____

What brings you joy?

○ _____

○ _____

○ _____

If you had free time during the day to do anything, what would you do?

○ _____

○ _____

○ _____

Make a List of Special Activities That You'd Love to Make Time For

_____ _____

_____ _____

_____ _____

_____ _____

_____ _____

Day 20: Make Time for You

Welcome to Day 20 of the 30-Day Productivity Challenge! Today's action step is to find ways to take time for you!

You work hard and you are striving to become as productive as possible. Now it's time to find ways to have more fun and enjoy life. Let go of feelings of guilt or pressure and prioritize time each day to do something fun, and each week to do something special, for you! What would you most enjoy doing? Turn to today's tracking sheet and have fun brainstorming and dreaming as you carve out time to enjoy life!

Turn the page for today's action pages.

At the end of the day, journal your *Daily Reflections* on the facing page. By prioritizing time to take action and reflect on your activity and results each day, you'll maximize the benefits you'll receive from this 30-Day Challenge.

Thought of the Day

"As you walk down the fairway of life
you must smell the roses,
for you only get to play one round."
—Ben Hogan

My Daily Reflections Journal
Day#_____   Date: _____

The Best Part of My Day: _____

_____

_____

_____

_____

Something New I Learned Today: _____

_____

_____

_____

_____

3 Things I'm Grateful For Today

◯ _____

◯ _____

◯ _____

Notes and Realizations

Take Time to Smell the Roses
You Work Hard and You Deserve to Enjoy Life!

How would you answer this question? "If I could do anything in the world, without feeling guilty, I would... _____

_____

_____

What would it be like to make it a priority to do something fun each day?

_____

_____

What would it feel like to take special time for you, each week? _____

_____

_____

Hobbies or Interests You'd Like to Pursue

_____   _____

_____   _____

_____   _____

_____   _____

_____   _____

Plan a Special Outing or Activity

_____

_____

_____

Plan and Schedule "Me" Time
Have Fun Planning Special Time for YOU!

Fun, Relaxing, or Pampering Activity: _____

_____

_____

Fun, Relaxing, or Pampering Activity: _____

_____

_____

Fun, Relaxing, or Pampering Activity: _____

_____

_____

Fun, Relaxing, or Pampering Activity: _____

_____

_____

Fun, Relaxing, or Pampering Activity: _____

_____

_____

Schedule These Activities Into Your Calendar

Date and Time: _____ Activity: _____

Date and Time: _____ Activity: _____

Date and Time: _____ Activity: _____

Date and Time: _____ Activity: _____

Date and Time: _____ Activity: _____

111

Day 21: Make Time for Family and Friends

Welcome to Day 21 of the 30-Day Productivity Challenge! Today's action step is to find ways to spend more time with the important people in your life.

With our busy schedules, it's easy to prioritize work related items and push aside making it a priority to spend time with family and friends. Turn the page to complete the *Make More Time for Family and Friends* page and find ways to carve out time for those who are most important in your life.

Turn the page for today's action pages.

At the end of the day, journal your *Daily Reflections* on the facing page. By prioritizing time to take action and reflect on your activity and results each day, you'll maximize the benefits you'll receive from this 30-Day Challenge.

Thought of the Day

"Once you replace negative thoughts with positive ones, you'll start having positive results."
—Willie Nelson

My Daily Reflections Journal
Day#_____   Date: _____

The Best Part of My Day: _____

_____

_____

_____

_____

Something New I Learned Today: _____

_____

_____

_____

_____

3 Things I'm Grateful For Today

○ _____

○ _____

○ _____

Notes and Realizations

Doodle - Brainstorm - Daydream

Friends I'd Like to Spend More Time With

Family I'd Like to Spend More Time With

Ways I Can Make Time to Be With The People Who Matter Most to Me

Make More Time for Family and Friends

Family Members I'd Like to Spend More Time With: _____

_____

_____

Activities and Fun Things We Can Do Together: _____

_____

_____

Friends I'd Most Like to Spend More Time With: _____

_____

_____

Activities and Fun Things We Can Do Together: _____

_____

_____

Ways I Can Make Time for the People Who Are Important to Me: _____

_____

_____

What I Need to Put in Place so I Can Spend More Time with Long-Distance Friends and Family: _____

_____

_____

Day 22: Write About What You Are Grateful For

Welcome to Day 22 of the 30-Day Productivity Challenge! Today's action step is to spend time reflecting on what you are grateful for.

Our lives are so busy that sometimes we forget to give thanks for what we have and who we are. With all the challenges that life brings us, it's easy to think about what is NOT working rather than think about what IS working. Turn to the *What I Am Grateful For* page and write about all the things you are grateful for.

Turn the page for today's action pages.

At the end of the day, journal your *Daily Reflections* on the facing page. By prioritizing time to take action and reflect on your activity and results each day, you'll maximize the benefits you'll receive from this 30-Day Challenge.

Thought of the Day

"Gratitude makes sense of our past, brings peace for today, and creates a vision for tomorrow."
—Melody Beattie

116

My Daily Reflections Journal
Day#_____   Date: _____

The Best Part of My Day: _____

_____

_____

_____

_____

Something New I Learned Today: _____

_____

_____

_____

_____

3 Things I'm Grateful For Today

○ _____

○ _____

○ _____

Notes and Realizations

Doodle - Brainstorm - Daydream

What I Am Grateful For

What is Working and Wonderful in My Life Is: _____

_____

_____

_____

_____

3 Things I'm Grateful For Regarding My Health

○ _____

○ _____

○ _____

3 Things I'm Grateful For Regarding My Family

○ _____

○ _____

○ _____

3 Things I'm Grateful For in My Personal Life

○ _____

○ _____

○ _____

3 Things I'm Grateful For in My Business

○ _____

○ _____

○ _____

Day 23: Make Time to Move Your Body

Welcome to Day 23 of the 30-Day Productivity Challenge! Today's action step is to find more ways to move your body.

In today's online world, it is easy to get sucked into spending hours at a time at the computer. It's important to make time to step away from the computer to stretch, breathe, and move your body. By making it a priority to move your body, you will find that you feel healthier and have more energy. Moving your body can also elevate your mood and your sense of well-being. Turn to the *I Make Time to Move My Body* page and have fun brainstorming ideas.

Turn the page for today's action pages.

At the end of the day, journal your *Daily Reflections* on the facing page. By prioritizing time to take action and reflect on your activity and results each day, you'll maximize the benefits you'll receive from this 30-Day Challenge.

Thought of the Day

"There's never enough time to do something right the first time, but there is always enough time to go back and do it again."
—Anonymous

My Daily Reflections Journal
Day#_____   Date: _____

The Best Part of My Day: _____

_____

_____

_____

_____

Something New I Learned Today: _____

_____

_____

_____

_____

3 Things I'm Grateful For Today

O _____

O _____

O _____

Notes and Realizations

Doodle - Brainstorm - Daydream

I Make Time to Move My Body

3 of My Favorite Outdoor Activies

○ _____
○ _____
○ _____

3 of My Favorite Indoor Activies

○ _____
○ _____
○ _____

Physical Activies I'd Like to Make More a Part of My Life

○ _____
○ _____
○ _____

What Holds Me Back From Getting More Exercise Is: _____

_____

_____

_____

Ideas for How I Can Make More Time to Move My Body: _____

_____

_____

_____

Day 24: Take Time to Dream

Welcome to Day 24 of the 30-Day Productivity Challenge! Today's action step is to spend time dreaming and writing about your heartfelt dreams.

What do you wish for? What do you hope for? What have you always wanted? By having dreams and putting a plan in place to achieve them, you will accomplish so much more. Spend some time thinking about (or remembering) what your dreams in life are. Consider posting images and positive affirmation statements about your dreams, where you can see them every day.

Turn the page for today's action pages.

At the end of the day, journal your *Daily Reflections* on the facing page. By prioritizing time to take action and reflect on your activity and results each day, you'll maximize the benefits you'll receive from this 30-Day Challenge.

Thought of the Day

"Lost wealth may be replaced by industry, lost knowledge by study, lost health by temperance or medicine, but lost time is gone forever."
—Samuel Smiles

My Daily Reflections Journal
Day#_____   Date: _____

The Best Part of My Day: _____

_____

_____

_____

_____

Something New I Learned Today: _____

_____

_____

_____

_____

3 Things I'm Grateful For Today

○ _____

○ _____

○ _____

Notes and Realizations

125

Doodle - Brainstorm - Daydream

Paste Images Here That Represent
Your Heartfelt Dreams

My Heartfelt Dreams

My Dream in Life is To: _____

_____

_____

If I Had $100,000 To Do Whatever I Want with I Woud: _____

_____

_____

If I Could Give Someone a Gift, of Any Value, I Would: _____

_____

_____

Here is a Positive Affirmation Statement About a Heartfelt Dream of Mine:

_____

_____

My Dream Wish List

_____   _____

_____   _____

_____   _____

_____   _____

Notes

Congratulations on Completing This Focus Area "Unplug and Take Time to Recharge"

Congratulations on completing Focus Area 4 of the 30-Day Productivity Challenge. These past 6 days we focused on unplugging and finding ways to recharge.

Throughout the week you had opportunities to:

- ☐ Make time to enjoy life
- ☐ Make time for you
- ☐ Make time for friends and family
- ☐ Spend time reflecting
- ☐ Give thought to your dreams and goals
- ☐ Make time to move your body

How does it feel to find more ways to enjoy life? _____

_____

_____

What can you do to make it a prioritiy to continue to find ways to enjoy life more?__

_____

_____

What special activity will you'll be focusing on during your next "me" time? _____

_____

_____

Hot Tip: Keep Having Fun

With all of the projects and tasks that come across your plate, it is so easy to keep pushing "having fun" time to the back burner. Consider scheduling fun time into your calendar on a daily and weekly basis and spend more time enjoying life. While having fun is important and essential, you don't want to have it disrupt your productivity. This said, consider using your fun and special time activities as rewards for a job well done!

129

Days
25-30

Streamline Social Media Systems

Notes

Week-at-a-Glance Six-Most-Important Things To-Do List

Day of the Week: _____

- ☐ _____
- ☐ _____
- ☐ _____
- ☐ _____
- ☐ _____
- ☐ _____

☐Exercise   ☐Drink Water
☐Have Fun   ☐Daily Reflections Journal

Day of the Week: _____

- ☐ _____
- ☐ _____
- ☐ _____
- ☐ _____
- ☐ _____
- ☐ _____

☐Exercise   ☐Drink Water
☐Have Fun   ☐Daily Reflections Journal

Day of the Week: _____

- ☐ _____
- ☐ _____
- ☐ _____
- ☐ _____
- ☐ _____
- ☐ _____

☐Exercise   ☐Drink Water
☐Have Fun   ☐Daily Reflections Journal

Day of the Week: _____

- ☐ _____
- ☐ _____
- ☐ _____
- ☐ _____
- ☐ _____
- ☐ _____

☐Exercise   ☐Drink Water
☐Have Fun   ☐Daily Reflections Journal

Day of the Week: _____

- ☐ _____
- ☐ _____
- ☐ _____
- ☐ _____
- ☐ _____
- ☐ _____

☐Exercise   ☐Drink Water
☐Have Fun   ☐Daily Reflections Journal

Day of the Week: _____

- ☐ _____
- ☐ _____
- ☐ _____
- ☐ _____
- ☐ _____
- ☐ _____

☐Exercise ☐Drink Water ☐Have Fun
☐Daily Reflections Journal

Today's Action Step

Day 25: Streamline Your Social Media Profiles

Welcome to Day 25 of the 30-Day Productivity Challenge! Today's action step is to streamline your social media profiles.

Check to make sure you are using the same headshot photograph on each network. This will expand your brand and allow you to become familiar to your audience. You'll also want to update your biography to ensure that your information is current. Turn to the *My Main Social Media Profiles* page and fill out the information. The main social media sites for authors are currently: Twitter, Facebook, LinkedIn, and Goodreads, though you may prefer different social networks.

Turn the page for today's action pages.

At the end of the day, journal your *Daily Reflections* on the facing page. By prioritizing time to take action and reflect on your activity and results each day, you'll maximize the benefits you'll receive from this 30-Day Challenge.

Thought of the Day

"The Internet is becoming the town square for the global village of tomorrow."
—Bill Gates

My Daily Reflections Journal
Day#_____   Date: _____

The Best Part of My Day: _____

_____

_____

_____

_____

Something New I Learned Today: _____

_____

_____

_____

_____

3 Things I'm Grateful For Today

O _____

O _____

O _____

Notes and Realizations

My Main Social Media Profiles

Name of Social Network: _____

What I Like Most About This Social Network: _____

_____

My Favorite Groups or Forums on This Site:

_____

_____

_____

Action Steps Checklist:

☐ I use the same photograph that I'm using on all social networks

☐ I've updated my biography

☐ I've schedule time, at least once a week, to spend on this site

Name of Social Network: _____

What I Like Most About This Social Network: _____

_____

My Favorite Groups or Forums on This Site:

_____

_____

_____

Action Steps Checklist:

☐ I use the same photograph that I'm using on all social networks

☐ I've updated my biography

136

☐ I've schedule time, at least once a week, to spend on this site

My Main Social Media Profiles

Name of Social Network: _____

What I Like Most About This Social Network: _____

_____

My Favorite Groups or Forums on This Site:

_____

_____

_____

Action Steps Checklist:

☐ I use the same photograph that I'm using on all social networks

☐ I've updated my biography

☐ I've schedule time, at least once a week, to spend on this site

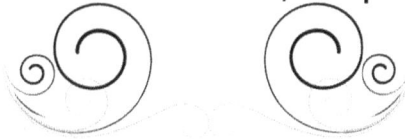

Name of Social Network: _____

What I Like Most About This Social Network: _____

_____

My Favorite Groups or Forums on This Site:

_____

_____

_____

Action Steps Checklist:

☐ I use the same photograph that I'm using on all social networks

☐ I've updated my biography

☐ I've schedule time, at least once a week, to spend on this site

Day 26: Harness the Power of Twitter Lists

Welcome to Day 26 of the 30-Day Productivity Challenge! Today's action step is to create Twitter lists.

As you may know, trying to access relevant content on Twitter is like trying to read billboards while speeding along the highway. By creating Twitter lists, you are able to more easily follow conversations on topics and by people of interest to you. To create a Twitter list, login to Twitter and search for people or keywords you are interested in. Click to follow people, then click on the gear image next to the "follow" button near their name, and add them to a list.

Turn the page for today's action pages.

At the end of the day, journal your *Daily Reflections* on the facing page. By prioritizing time to take action and reflect on your activity and results each day, you'll maximize the benefits you'll receive from this 30-Day Challenge.

Thought of the Day

"Getting information off the Internet is like taking a drink from a fire hydrant."
—Mitch Kapor

My Daily Reflections Journal
Day#_____   Date: _____

The Best Part of My Day: _____

_____

_____

_____

_____

Something New I Learned Today: _____

_____

_____

_____

_____

3 Things I'm Grateful For Today

○ _____

○ _____

○ _____

Notes and Realizations

My Top Twitter Lists

Name of List: _____

Why I've Created This List: _____

The Top Three People I've Added to This List

Their Name: _____   Their Twitter ID: _____

Their Name: _____   Their Twitter ID: _____

Their Name: _____   Their Twitter ID: _____

Name of List: _____

Why I've Created This List: _____

The Top Three People I've Added to This List

Their Name: _____   Their Twitter ID: _____

Their Name: _____   Their Twitter ID: _____

Their Name: _____   Their Twitter ID: _____

Name of List: _____

Why I've Created This List: _____

The Top Three People I've Added to This List

Their Name: _____   Their Twitter ID: _____

Their Name: _____   Their Twitter ID: _____

Their Name: _____   Their Twitter ID: _____

My Top Twitter Lists

Name of List: _____

Why I've Created This List: _____

The Top Three People I've Added to This List

Their Name: _____   Their Twitter ID: _____

Their Name: _____   Their Twitter ID: _____

Their Name: _____   Their Twitter ID: _____

Name of List: _____

Why I've Created This List: _____

The Top Three People I've Added to This List

Their Name: _____   Their Twitter ID: _____

Their Name: _____   Their Twitter ID: _____

Their Name: _____   Their Twitter ID: _____

Name of List: _____

Why I've Created This List: _____

The Top Three People I've Added to This List

Their Name: _____   Their Twitter ID: _____

Their Name: _____   Their Twitter ID: _____

Their Name: _____   Their Twitter ID: _____

Day 27: Automate Social Media with Hootsuite

Welcome to Day 27 of the 30-Day Productivity Challenge! Today's action step is to automate social media with Hootsuite.com

Create a free account, connect your social profiles, create tabs and streams in order to access content, and schedule tweets and posts to go out to the social networks. Visit Hootsuite's "product support" tab to view tutorials. By streamlining your social media activities, you'll save time while being able to become more active and engaged. Turn to today's action pages and map out your tabs and streams, and compose tweets to go out from your Hootsuite dashboard.

Turn the page for today's action pages.

At the end of the day, journal your *Daily Reflections* on the facing page. By prioritizing time to take action and reflect on your activity and results each day, you'll maximize the benefits you'll receive from this 30-Day Challenge.

Thought of the Day

"One of the Internet's strengths is its ability to help consumers find the right needle in a digital haystack of data."
—Jared Sandberg

My Daily Reflections Journal
Day#_____   Date: _____

The Best Part of My Day: _____

_____

_____

_____

_____

Something New I Learned Today: _____

_____

_____

_____

_____

3 Things I'm Grateful For Today

○ _____

○ _____

○ _____

Notes and Realizations

Collection of Tweets to Schedule in Hootsuite
Remember to Add URLs When Appropriate

Tweet an Inspiring Quote: _____

_____

_____

Tweet About Your Latest Blog Post: _____

_____

_____

Tweet About Something Positive in the News: _____

_____

_____

Tweet About _____: _____

_____

_____

Tweet About _____: _____

_____

_____

My Hootsuite Tabs and Streams

Title for Tab #1: _____

Type of Content to Feature in This Stream:_____

_____

Content Topic for Stream #1: _____

Content Topic for Stream #2: _____

Content Topic for Stream #3: _____

Title for Tab #2: _____

Type of Content to Feature in This Stream:_____

_____

Content Topic for Stream #1: _____

Content Topic for Stream #2: _____

Content Topic for Stream #3: _____

Title for Tab #3: _____

Type of Content to Feature in This Stream:_____

_____

Content Topic for Stream #1: _____

Content Topic for Stream #2: _____

Content Topic for Stream #3: _____

Day 28: Share Inspiring Thoughts on Facebook

Welcome to Day 28 of the 30-Day Productivity Challenge! Today's action step is to share inspiring thoughts on Facebook.

This can be in the form of quotes, realizations, inspirations, or images with inspiring quotes added to them. By including a photograph with your post, you will get more engagement and people are more likely to read what you have written. You can find collections of inspiring quotes on sites such as BrainyQuotes.com. Turn to today's action pages and plan out ideas for inspiring thoughts you'd like to share on Facebook.

Turn the page for today's action pages.

At the end of the day, journal your *Daily Reflections* on the facing page. By prioritizing time to take action and reflect on your activity and results each day, you'll maximize the benefits you'll receive from this 30-Day Challenge.

Thought of the Day

"The secret to social media success is to think and act like a member first, and a marketer second."
—Mari Smith

My Daily Reflections Journal
Day#_____   Date: _____

The Best Part of My Day: _____

_____

_____

_____

_____

Something New I Learned Today: _____

_____

_____

_____

_____

3 Things I'm Grateful For Today

○ _____

○ _____

○ _____

Notes and Realizations

Inspiring Quotes and Thoughts
Add Inspiring Quotes or Thoughts in the Spaces Provided Below

Inspiring Quotes and Thoughts
Add Inspiring Quotes or Thoughts in the Spaces Provided Below

Day 29: Schedule Time to Socialize

Welcome to Day 29 of the 30-Day Productivity Challenge! Today's action step is to schedule time in your calendar for socializing on the social networks.

When you don't schedule time to socialize, you'll either end up spending way too much time on social media sites, or you won't be able to find the time to get there. Give thought to the best time of week and the best times of day for you to network and share ideas on the social media sites. Open your calendar and schedule one or more consistent times throughout the week to socialize online. Set these as recurring appointments so you develop consistency.

Turn the page for today's action pages.

At the end of the day, journal your *Daily Reflections* on the facing page. By prioritizing tIme to take action and reflect on your activity and results each day, you'll maximize the benefits you'll receive from this 30-Day Challenge.

Thought of the Day

"Social media is changing the way we communicate and the way we are perceived, both positively and negatively. Every time you post a photo, or update your status, you are contributing to your own digital footprint and personal brand."
—Amy Jo Martin

My Daily Reflections Journal
Day#_____   Date: _____

The Best Part of My Day: _____

_____

_____

_____

_____

Something New I Learned Today: _____

_____

_____

_____

_____

3 Things I'm Grateful For Today

○ _____

○ _____

○ _____

Notes and Realizations

My Favorite Online Groups and Forums

Group or Forum Name: _____

URL: _____

Focus of Group or Forum: _____

What I Enjoy Most About This Group: _____

_____

Names of people I most enjoy connecting with in this group:

_____   _____

_____   _____

_____   _____

Group or Forum Name: _____

URL: _____

Focus of Group or Forum: _____

What I Enjoy Most About This Group: _____

_____

Names of people I most enjoy connecting with in this group:

_____   _____

_____   _____

_____   _____

My Favorite Online Groups and Forums

Group or Forum Name: _____

URL: _____

Focus of Group or Forum: _____

What I Enjoy Most About This Group: _____

_____

Names of people I most enjoy connecting with in this group:

_____   _____

_____   _____

_____   _____

Group or Forum Name: _____

URL: _____

Focus of Group or Forum: _____

What I Enjoy Most About This Group: _____

_____

Names of people I most enjoy connecting with in this group:

_____   _____

_____   _____

_____   _____

Day 30: Enjoy Open-Ended Internet Time

Welcome to Day 30 of the 30-Day Productivity Challenge! Today's action step is to carve out time in your busy schedule to enjoy open-ended time on the Internet.

Open up your calendar and schedule a recurring time that you'll allow yourself to have fun exploring our online universe. Weekends or after business hours are typically the best times for this as you are more likely to feel free to explore, read, research, and enjoy "blowing with the wind" as you enjoy the wonderful worldwide web.

Turn the page for today's action pages.

At the end of the day, journal your *Daily Reflections* on the facing page. By prioritizing time to take action and reflect on your activity and results each day, you'll maximize the benefits you'll receive from this 30-Day Challenge.

Thought of the Day

*"Give a person a fish and you feed them for a day;
teach that person to use the Internet
and they won't bother you for weeks."*
—Author Unknown

My Daily Reflections Journal
Day#_____   Date: _____

The Best Part of My Day: _____

_____

_____

_____

_____

Something New I Learned Today: _____

_____

_____

_____

_____

3 Things I'm Grateful For Today

○ _____

○ _____

○ _____

Notes and Realizations

My Open-Ended Internet Time Journal
Make Note of the Interesting Websites That You Travel To

Name of Website: _____

URL of Website: _____

What Interested Me: _____

Name of Website: _____

URL of Website: _____

What Interested Me: _____

Name of Website: _____

URL of Website: _____

What Interested Me: _____

Name of Website: _____

URL of Website: _____

What Interested Me: _____

Name of Website: _____

URL of Website: _____

What Interested Me: _____

My Open-Ended Internet Time Journal
Make Note of the Insteresting Articles You Discover

Title of Article: _____

URL to Article: _____

My Thoughts About This Article _____

_____

Title of Article: _____

URL to Article: _____

My Thoughts About This Article _____

_____

Title of Article: _____

URL to Article: _____

My Thoughts About This Article _____

_____

Title of Article: _____

URL to Article: _____

My Thoughts About This Article _____

_____

Notes

Congratulations on Completing This Focus Area "Streamline Your Social Media Systems"

Congratulations on completing Focus Area 5 of the 30-Day Productivity Challenge. These past 6 days we focused on streamlining your social media systems.

Throughout the week you had opportunities to:

- ☐ Streamline your social media profiles
- ☐ Harness the power of Twitter lists
- ☐ Automate social media with Hootsuite
- ☐ Share inspiring thoughts on Facebook
- ☐ Schedule time to socialize
- ☐ Enjoy open-ended Internet time

How does it feel to have more control over your social media time and activities? ___

_____

_____

What are you enjoying most about your "blow with the wind" Internet time? _____

_____

_____

How will you monitor the time you spend on the social networks? _____

_____

_____

Hot Tip: Have Fun Socializing

In many ways, the Internet has become the modern day community center. By finding productive ways to participate in online groups, you'll have opportunities to network, ask questions, share ideas, and develop new friendships. By scheduling time to socialize you'll be able to make it a priority to participate in the social networks. By adhering to these scheduled times, you'll also be able to maintain healthy boundaries around your work and family time.

30-Day Challenge Wrap Up and Reflections

Congratulations! You have completed the 30-Day Productivity Challenge!

Now that you've streamlined your systems, found ways to become more productive, and have prioritized ways to have more fun and enjoyment in your life, find ways to keep the momentum going.

Consider scheduling a time each week to check in with yourself and reflect on your habits and accomplishments.

- ☐ Are you prioritizing "me" time and "family and friends" time?
- ☐ Are you maintaining your new email checking habits?
- ☐ Are you prioritizing writing time?

Know that this guide is here for you as a tool and a reference. You can review exercises from time to time, or you can make it a priority to read a tip-a-day from this guide, to reinforce the new success-focused habits you've created.

Turn to the next page and take a moment to jot down ideas for how you will keep the momentum going.

Wishing you much happiness and dreams come true!

Here's to your success,
D'vorah

Ways I Can Keep the Momentum Going

Ways I'll Continue to Make Becoming More Producitive a Priority

○ _____

○ _____

○ _____

Ways I'll Continue to Use the Brain Dump and Six-Most-Important Pages

○ _____

○ _____

○ _____

Ways I'll Continue to Tame the Email Dragon

○ _____

○ _____

○ _____

Ways I'll Continue to Prioritize "Me" Time and "Friends and Family" Time

○ _____

○ _____

○ _____

Notes - Ideas - Reflections: _____

_____

_____

Notes

Next Steps

About D'vorah

D'vorah Lansky, M.Ed., is the bestselling author of several books including; *Book Marketing Made Easy: Simple Strategies for Selling Your Nonfiction Book* Online and the *Productivity Action Guide for Authors: 90 Days to a More Productive You.*

She is also the founder and producer of the Annual Book Marketing Conference Online. This year marks the 10th year of this event!

Through her coaching and training programs, D'vorah has taught thousands of authors how to effectively and affordably market their books online.

Books by D'vorah

Check out all of D'vorah's books at: www.BooksByDvorah.com

Her flagship book is *Book Marketing Made Easy: Simple Strategies for Selling Your Nonfiction Book Online.* Discover the secrets that successful authors use to market their books online.

In *Book Marketing Made Easy* you will learn how to: increase your credibility and be seen as an expert in your field, sell more books to people who will benefit from your message, create multiple sources of income with the content of your book, harness the power of multimedia marketing to reach more people, and use social media to increase your influence and expand your market.

$14.95
Available on Amazon.com or a bookstore near you!
ISBN: 978-0965197595

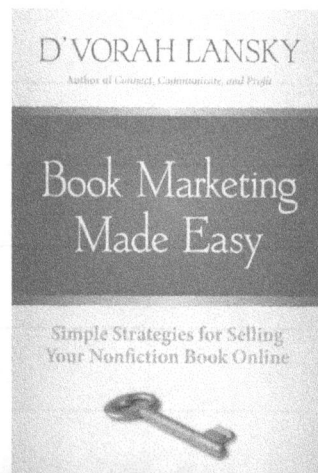

D'VORAH LANSKY
Author of Connect, Communicate, and Profit

Book Marketing
Made Easy

Simple Strategies for Selling
Your Nonfiction Book Online

Take Your Productivity Further

Leverage the Lessons You've Learned in this Action Guide!

Join D'vorah and a group of success-focused authors
for an interactive, power-packed experience!

Enjoy a well-rounded productivity system for accomplishing any goal!

In the 30-Day Productivity Challenge for Authors **online course**, you can go from overwhelmed to becoming more productive than you ever believed possible! Enjoy hands-on training, step-by-step instruction, group interaction, and personalized support in a safe and nurturing environment.

By participating in this program you'll receive:

- ✿ 30 days of daily productivity tips, weekly videos, and guest expert workshops!
- ✿ Access to our interactive discussion forum, where you'll be able to connect with other authors and get your questions answered!
- ✿ Lifetime access to the program, so you can learn and take action when it's convenient for you!
- ✿ A personalized action plan, created by you - for you, that you can use in your life and business!

This program is available on-demand so there are no dates to worry about.

Join us for the
30-Day Productivity Challenge for Authors at:
www.ReachMoreReaders.com/productive

www.ingramcontent.com/pod-product-compliance
Lightning Source LLC
Chambersburg PA
CBHW080509110426

42742CB00017B/3054